# US Policy Toward Putin's Russia

*A hearing before the House Committee on Foreign Affairs*

William Dunkerley

Published by
Omnicom Press
New Britain, CT, USA
*Publishers since 1981*

www.OmnicomPress.com

ISBN-13: 978-1979535281
ISBN-10: 1979535280
Printed in the United States of America

*US Policy Toward Putin's Russia is part of the "Russia: Straight Talk on Hushed Issues" monograph series. It is dedicated to the concept of a safe, sustaining, and positive relationship between the United States and the Russian Federation.*


*A list of other monographs in this series can be found at:*

*www.OmnicomPress.com/monographs*

# CONTENTS

This monograph presents a transcript of a House of Representatives hearing on the subject of "US Policy Toward Putin's Russia." (An appendix to the monograph appears at the end of the transcript.)

I personally viewed the video recording of the proceedings and wish to issue this forewarning: As you read the transcript, be aware that the quality of evidence introduced by Members and witnesses may vary considerably with regard to factualness. I strongly recommend that you fact check any statements that are of particular interest to you.

My own detailed analysis of the hearing is presented in a monograph titled *Congress Warned Over Russia*. That publication also contains my written statement that was introduced into the official record of the hearing.

# U.S. POLICY TOWARD PUTIN'S RUSSIA

HEARING BEFORE THE COMMITTEE ON
FOREIGN AFFAIRS

HOUSE OF REPRESENTATIVES

ONE HUNDRED FOURTEENTH CONGRESS

SECOND SESSION
JUNE 14, 2016

# COMMITTEE ON FOREIGN AFFAIRS

EDWARD R. ROYCE, California, Chairman
CHRISTOPHER H. SMITH, New Jersey*
ELIOT L. ENGEL, New York
ILEANA ROS-LEHTINEN, Florida*
BRAD SHERMAN, California
DANA ROHRABACHER, California
GREGORY W. MEEKS, New York
STEVE CHABOT, Ohio
ALBIO SIRES, New Jersey*
JOE WILSON, South Carolina
GERALD E. CONNOLLY, Virginia
MICHAEL T. MCCAUL, Texas*
THEODORE E. DEUTCH, Florida*
TED POE, Texas*
BRIAN HIGGINS, New York*
MATT SALMON, Arizona*

KAREN BASS, California
DARRELL E. ISSA, California*
WILLIAM KEATING, Massachusetts*
TOM MARINO, Pennsylvania
DAVID CICILLINE, Rhode Island
JEFF DUNCAN, South Carolina*
ALAN GRAYSON, Florida*
MO BROOKS, Alabama*
AMI BERA, California*
PAUL COOK, California*
ALAN S. LOWENTHAL, California*
RANDY K. WEBER SR., Texas*
GRACE MENG, New York*
SCOTT PERRY, Pennsylvania*
LOIS FRANKEL, Florida*
RON DESANTIS, Florida*
TULSI GABBARD, Hawaii*
MARK MEADOWS, North Carolina*
JOAQUIN CASTRO, Texas*
TED S. YOHO, Florida*
ROBIN L. KELLY, Illinois*
CURT CLAWSON, Florida*
BRENDAN F. BOYLE, Pennsylvania*
SCOTT DESJARLAIS, Tennessee*
REID J. RIBBLE, Wisconsin*
DAVID A. TROTT, Michigan
LEE M. ZELDIN, New York
DANIEL DONOVAN, New York*

*Absent. Did not attend hearing.

**STAFF**

AMY PORTER, Chief of Staff
THOMASSHEEHY, Staff Director
JASON STEINBAUM, Democratic Staff Director

**WITNESSES**

The Honorable Michael McFaul, senior fellow
and director at the Freeman Spogli Institute for
International Studies, Stanford University
(former American Ambassador to Russia)

The Honorable Jack Matlock, fellow, Rubenstein
Fellows Academy, Duke University (former
American Ambassador to the U.S.S.R)

Leon Aron, Ph.D., resident scholar and director
of Russian Studies, The American Enterprise
Institute

## TUESDAY, JUNE 14, 2016

The committee met, pursuant to notice, at 10:11 a.m., in room 2172, Rayburn House Office Building, Hon. Edward Royce (chairman of the committee) presiding.

Chairman ROYCE. The committee will come to order. I will ask all our members to take their seats.

Winston Churchill famously described Russia as "a riddle wrapped in a mystery inside an enigma," but I think for many of us, less well-known is what he said next, because he commented about unlocking that riddle. He said, "But perhaps there is a key. And that key is Russian national interest."

The problem is that we are not dealing with the interests of the Russian people. We could be if we were broadcasting into Russia the way we did during the Reagan administration when we had that message about political pluralism and tolerance and that message of educating people effectively on what was going on inside Russia and around the world. But we don't.

Instead, we are dealing with the interests of Vladimir Putin, because he is in a position there where he is calling the shots. And he has not demonstrated much interest in cooperating with the United States. In fact, many of his policies are directly undermining America-from selling advanced weapons to Iran to destabilizing our allies by sending waves of Syrian refugees, over several million now, across their borders. And for the first time since the end of the Cold War, we have seen a situation where we have been forced to increase our military presence in Europe to make clear our readiness to defend NATO.

Yet, in this environment, Putin continues to escalate. That is why we have this hearing today on our U.S. policy toward Putin's Russia. Over the past year, he has repeatedly sent Russian warplanes to buzz U.S. ships and planes in international waters. These are reckless acts, these are provocative acts, and a miscalculation could easily result in direct confrontation.

As this committee has examined, Russia's propaganda machine- and for any of you who have watched RT television, you can see how it has a constant stream of disinformation that it puts out about the United States, about the U.K., about what actually happens in the world. But that machinery, under Putin, is in overdrive. It is undermining governments, including NATO allies. And, meanwhile, back in Russia, independent media and dissidents are forcefully sidelined. And for the media, when I say "forcibly," I mean imprisoned or sometimes shot.

A big part of the problem is that the administration has repeatedly rushed to try to cooperate with Russia, beginning with a string of one-sided concessions in the New START arms-control agreement. I would just point out, when we pulled out the interceptor system in Poland and in the Czech Republic, I think that was a blunder. We were quick to join diplomatic efforts in Syria, even as the opposition forces we support have come under repeated Russian aerial attack. And this has convinced the Russians that, once again, the administration will concede a great deal for very little in return for the concession.

That does not mean that we should rule out cooperation with Russia. We should cooperate with Russia. But cooperation means benefits for both sides. A tougher and more consistent approach on our part might convince Putin that cooperation is more advantageous than the reflexive confrontation that he often resorts to. We have clearly demonstrated that we are open to cooperation. It is Putin who is not. And if he continues playing a zero-sum game and regards the U.S. as an enemy to achieving his ends, then the possibility of compromise is zero under that circumstance. Much of his behavior to date fits that description, most glaringly seen by his invasion of Ukraine and what happened in Georgia.

Unfortunately, Putin has repeatedly calculated-rightfully so- that the administration's response to his aggression will be lackluster. The U.S., in cooperation with the EU and others, has imposed sanctions, which have resulted in significant pressure on the Russian economy, but the administration has refused to provide Ukraine, for example, with the anti-tank weaponry needed to stop Russian tanks, which can only be interpreted in Moscow as weakness.

The tragedy is that there are many problems where both countries could benefit from cooperation. One of the most obvious is combating Islamist terrorism. One witness today has intensely studied its rapid spread in Russia and in Central Asia, which, together, provide the largest number of recruits for ISIS outside of the Arab countries.

Putin says he is genuinely concerned about the rising threat. In fact, that was his stated goal in intervening in Syria. But, as we know, his real agenda was to save the Assad regime, which has meant targeting the opposition forces that are supported by the U.S. far more than any targeting of ISIS forces.

It is clear that U.S. strategies to deal with Russia have failed. If we want to accomplish a different result, we must negotiate from a position of strength. Only then will cooperation be possible with a man who has demonstrated that the hope of cooperation cannot survive the cold calculation of his narrow interests.

And one way to address this, to get back to a theme that I have pushed for a number of years here with my colleague Eliot Engel, is the legislation that Eliot and I have advanced to try to get back to a program, as we once had with Radio Free Europe, which we should be doing with social media, with television. We should be broadcasting into Russia, telling Russians what is actually going on in their society, explaining to Russians what is happening around the world, explaining the issue of tolerance, of political pluralism, of these perceptions that the rest of the world have, and the truth. If Putin is going to continue to put out disinformation and misinformation and lie about the West, at the very least we could be telling the truth about what is happening inside Russia to Russians so that the people have a better understanding of this situation. I now turn to Ranking Member Eliot Engel of New York for any comments he may have.

Mr. ENGEL. Thank you very much, Mr. Chairman. And let me say I agree with the statement you just made. Thank you for calling this hearing. You and I have long shared deep concerns about Russia's aggression under Vladimir Putin, and I am grateful that you have focused the committee's attention on this challenge. To all of our witnesses, welcome to the Foreign Affairs Committee. We are grateful for your expertise and insight.

Ambassador McFaul, let me say how particularly impressed I was with your service as our top diplomat in Moscow. I know you were the target of all sorts of absurd accusations and harassment by Putin's allies, and I know that you were never afraid to push back against misinformation and stand your ground. And you are exactly the kind of diplomat we need to meet 21st-century challenges, so thank you for your service.

And the other witnesses, thank you, as well, for your service. I have come to view Putin's Russia as a unique challenge on the global stage. When we face crises around the world, we often ask ourselves, "What could we have done differently?" or, "What are the opportunities to defuse the situation?" But, with Putin, there may not be answers to those questions because he is playing by his own set of rules.

Putin has ignored Russian law, cracking down on the human rights of Russia's people and literally robbing future generations of their prosperity. He has destroyed Russia's standing in the world, walking away from the country's international obligations and shoring up the brutal Assad regime in Syria. And he has threatened the norms that have largely kept the peace in Europe since World War II, trampling on the sovereignty of Russia's neighbors, testing the resolve of NATO, and working to undermine Western unity.

I want to be careful not to conflate Putin and his corrupt leadership with the Russian people. Russia is a great nation, but Putin is not Russia. He is an unapologetic, authoritarian kleptocrat, a grave threat to his own people and to stability and security across Europe and beyond.

So how do we craft a policy to deal with such an unpredictable and irresponsible leader? For now, the best approach seems to be one of geographical containment. We cannot fix what is ailing Russian society, but we can try to keep it within Russia's recognized borders.

This may be a great test for NATO's role in the 21st century. NATO, of course, has no ambition to chip away at Russia's territory, but I am confident that the alliance will keep its Article 5 promise. Putin uses lies and confusion to cast doubt on NATO's ability, so I am glad that NATO is ramping up its presence in Eastern Europe, sending a clear signal that the alliance will not back down in the face of Putin's aggression.

I believe and I have said for a long time that I think NATO is being tested. And if we fail the test, I think it the end of the alliance. We cannot fail the test.

Aside from that, sanctions have given us mixed results. As violence in eastern Ukraine escalates again, it is clear that sanctions haven't done enough to thwart Putin's ambitions. But sanctions are better than nothing, and, in the long term, I believe we have weakened Putin's ability to project a destabilizing force beyond Russia's borders.

But we know Putin isn't going anywhere, so we are left to ask, what else should we be doing?

I recently introduced legislation that, in my view, would take us in the right direction. My bill, the STAND for Ukraine Act, would tighten sanctions

on Russia and would reject any form of
recognition of Russia's rule over Crimea in the
same way we didn't recognize Soviet occupation
of the Baltic states during the Cold War. It would
also help to drive investment in Ukraine and push
back against Russian propaganda and
disinformation.

There are other issues I hope we can touch on
today, as well: How do we help the Russian
people hear a different point of view? And the
chairman spoke about that in his opening
statement. After all, Putin's apparent approval
ratings have a lot to do with the fact that there is
simply no alternative. How do we seize on the
common ground we share with the citizens of
Russia? Even if the United States isn't popular in
Russia, we know that the country's citizens are
disgusted by corruption at every level of
government. And let me close by saying we are
not focusing on Russia today because we want to
pick a fight, breathe new life into old animosities,
or drag the country down. A failed Russia would
spread damaging ripple effects around the world.
Rather, we hold out hope for the people of
Russia. We want to see them realize their
democratic aspirations. We want to see their
country become a stable and prosperous
European power and partner on the world stage.
Putin has strangled democracy in Russia. We had

such high hopes. But I look forward to hearing our witnesses today and hearing what they have to say, and I thank them again for coming. And I yield back, Mr. Chairman.

Chairman ROYCE. All right. This morning, we are pleased to be joined by a distinguished panel. The Honorable Michael McFaul is a professor at Stanford University. Prior to his position, Ambassador McFaul served 5 years in the Obama administration, first as Special Assistant to the President and Senior Director for Russia and Eurasia at the National Security Council, and then as the U.S. Ambassador to Russia. Ambassador Jack Matlock is a fellow at Duke University, and, prior to this position, Ambassador Matlock served 35 years in the American Foreign Service. During that time, he has served as the Ambassador to the Soviet Union, Special Assistant to the President for National Security Affairs, and Ambassador to Czechoslovakia from 1981 to 1983. Dr. Leon Aron is a resident scholar and director of Russian studies at the American Enterprise Institute. He has served on the Broadcasting Board of Governors since 2015. Prior to these positions, he taught at Georgetown University. Without objection, the witnesses' full prepared statements will be made part of the record, and our members will have 5 calendar days to submit statements and questions and extraneous material for the record. Ambassador McFaul, please summarize your remarks, if you could. Thank you, Ambassador.

STATEMENT OF THE HONORABLE MICHAEL MCFAUL, SENIOR FELLOW AND DIRECTOR AT THE FREEMAN SPOGLI INSTITUTE FOR INTERNATIONAL STUDIES, STANFORD UNIVERSITY (FORMER AMERICAN AMBASSADOR TO RUSSIA)

Ambassador MCFAUL. Thank you, Mr. Chairman. Thank you--

Chairman ROYCE. Ambassador, let me just interrupt you. If everyone would push that red button.

Ambassador MCFAUL. Push the top button?

Chairman ROYCE. There you go.

Ambassador MCFAUL. All right? There you go. So I will thank you again, Chairman Royce and Ranking Member Engel and other members of the committee, including several of you that I had the pleasure of hosting in Moscow when I was Ambassador.

It is great to be back with Ambassador Matlock and Leon Aron, people I know well. I guarantee you, if you listen, you are going to learn something from these two gentlemen today.

I have a longer report that I want to put in the record, but I just want to answer two questions today in the limited time I have: Why did we get here, how did we get here, in terms of this confrontation, which I believe is worse than at any time since the Cold War? In fact, I think you have to go deep into the Cold War to see a time that has been so confrontational. And, as the Russians like to say, "Chto delat," what is to be done.

And I want to focus on the diagnostics first, in part because I am an aspiring professor, recovering bureaucrat, and I think it is important to know the "why" question before you do the prescription. So I am going to first focus on that and, in my limited time, then get to prescriptions.

One argument why we are in this mess that we are in today is that Russia, and Putin in particular, is pushing back after decades of American aggression against him. The United States lectured Russia about markets and democracy, we expanded NATO, we bombed Serbia, we invaded Iraq, we supported color revolutions, so the argument goes, and so Putin just had to push back; he was compelled to annex Crimea and intervene in eastern Ukraine. And most certainly that is the main conflict that has sparked the confrontation.

Now, I want to be clear. None of those policies were popular in Moscow during the last three decades, although it should be noted that both President Yeltsin and Putin at one point flirted with the idea of actually joining NATO.

But in between that negative record that I just described and our moment today, there was a period of cooperation. We in the Obama administration called it the "reset." And, during that period, we got a lot of things done that, Mr. Chairman, in my opinion, were in the American national interests. We got the START Treaty done. We got sanctions on Iran. We expanded the northern distribution network to supply our troops in Afghanistan so we had an alternative route instead of Pakistan, which was vital to a military mission we had in 2011 when we killed Osama bin Laden. We got them into the World Trade Organization. We got them to support U.N. Security Council Resolutions 1970 and 1973 on Libya. And we increased trade and investment during that period. By the way, during this period, 60 percent of Americans thought Russia

**24**

was a friendly or allied country, and vice versa inside Russia.

That was just 4 years ago. That wasn't 40 years ago or before the Bolshevik revolution. So you can't explain the period of cooperation that I just described looking at these previous variables. Something else has to be here.

A second explanation is that Obama was weak and created the permissive conditions for Putin's aggression. Maybe we will have time to talk about that in questions and answers in more detail. I would just remind you that every time a Russian leader has decided to use force or to suppress democratic movements in Eastern Europe, the United States has not had good options for deterring it. Whether it is in Georgia in 2008 under George W. Bush, the crackdown on Solidarity in 1981 under Ronald Reagan, 1968 in Czechoslovakia, or 1966 in Hungary, we did not have military means for stopping them.

Let me say something really provocative. I believe the Obama administration's response looks more like Ronald Reagan's response to what happened in Poland in 1981 than George Bush's response to what happened in Georgia in 2008. That did get your attention, didn't it? I will bet you we are going to come back with that. The third explanation, and what I think is the real driving explanation for what is going on, is this is all about domestic politics in Russia and in Ukraine and very little to do with American foreign policy, either strong or weak. Two things are important to this explanation. One, Putin returned. And Putin is not Medvedev. He sees the world in zero-sum terms. He sees the hand of the CIA in fomenting revolutions in the Arab world, in Ukraine, and in Russia. And he sees us fundamentally as an enemy. And, second, there were giant demonstrations against his regime in December 2011 and in the spring of 2012 when I was Ambassador, and he needed a new argument to suppress those people, to say that they were the enemies of the regime. And that is when he rolled out this old playbook from the Soviet era and described us-the United States, the Obama administration, and me personally-as the enemy, those that are fomenting revolution against him.

And, in that context, there is not an easy way to cooperate with him if he sees the world in these zero-sum terms and if he sees an American hand behind these uprisings, be they in Moscow or Kiev. So, to me, I actually agree with both the previous statements. It is a tragic moment in U.S.-Russian relations; I don't celebrate this at all. But we have to have a patient, comprehensive policy for deterring Russian aggression, working with the government when it is in our national interest, and supporting Russian society. In my written remarks, I go into detail about a six-point plan. Let me just mention the headlines and then stop. One, most important of all, in my opinion, to deter Putin's aggression, is to help Ukrainian democracy and markets succeed. Nothing else is more important than that objective, and so I look forward to seeing your legislation. I think that is orders of magnitude more important than anything else. Second, strengthening NATO, as has already been noted. I fully concur with that. Third, pushing back on Russian propaganda, not through American propaganda but through facts. I agree with that. Fourth, working with the government in limited ways when we can, when it serves our national interest. And, finally, engaging in supporting the Russian people, because there is no reason to contain both the state and the people. We should continue to engage when the circumstances allow. Thank you, Mr. Chairman.

Chairman ROYCE. Thank you, Ambassador McFaul. Now we will go to Ambassador Jack Matlock.

STATEMENT OF THE HONORABLE JACK MATLOCK, FELLOW, RUBENSTEIN FELLOWS ACADEMY, DUKE UNIVERSITY

(FORMER AMERICAN AMBASSADOR TO THE U.S.S.R)

Ambassador MATLOCK. Mr. Chairman, members of the committee, thank you for your invitation to join these distinguished scholars.

Chairman ROYCE. Ambassador, I am going to suggest you pull that microphone closer. There you go. Thank you, sir.

Ambassador MATLOCK. All right.

Thank you for your invitation. And I am very pleased to join these distinguished scholars in discussing our relations with Russia. Ambassador McFaul coauthored, among his other works, a fine book which I make a required reading for my students of U.S.-Russian relations. And he, of course, was Ambassador to Russia. And I would have to say that I don't know whether it was an advantage or disadvantage, but he had a larger staff to deal with Russia than I had to deal with the entire Soviet Union. So I don't know whether that was a blessing or a curse, except that I had, I think, the best staff anyone could wish at the time that we were dealing with the Soviet Union. And, of course, Dr. Aron and I go back a long way in many different meetings and so on. So I am very happy to be here along with them.

Some of my perceptions are going to be probably different, because I am deeply concerned with the direction U.S.-Russian relations have taken of late. We can debate-and I will participate in it if we wish-what caused this. I have written extensively on it. And I would simply say that the perception on both sides, in both cases, I think, has distortions. Theirs may be greater or lesser than ours, but there is cause and effect in the interaction that went both ways.

The mutual accusations and public acrimony has at times been reminiscent of that at the height or the depth of the Cold War, but the issues are quite different.

The Cold War was fundamentally about ideology, the attempt of the Communist-ruled Soviet Union to spread its control of other countries by encouraging what Karl Marx had called proletarian revolutions against existing governments. The Soviet leaders called their system socialist, but it actually was state monopoly capitalism that tried to replace market forces with government fiat. It was a catastrophic failure in meeting people's needs, but it managed to build a formidable and, in some respect, unmatched military power.

Today's tensions are not about ideology. Russia is

now a capitalist country. Okay, one that has more state control than many others, but basically capitalist. It is not trying to spread communism in the world. Today's tensions, if we really look at them objectively, are more like those that, through incredible misjudgment, brought on World War I-that is, competition for control of territory in and outside Europe.

We know how that ended. Every European country involved suffered more than they could possibly have gained. Competition over territory was bad enough a century ago. Since World War II, however, the danger has risen exponentially if countries with nuclear weapons stumble into military conflict. The number of nuclear weapons that remain in U.S. and Russian arsenals represent a potential existential threat to every nation on Earth, including specifically both Russia and the United States.

So how did we end the Cold War and reduce this threat? One key element was an agreement that President Ronald Reagan and General Secretary Mikhail Gorbachev made in their very first meeting. They agreed on a statement that Reagan had made in two previous speeches: A nuclear war cannot be won and must never be fought. And then they added, since both countries are nuclear powers: That means there can be no war between us.

With that statement agreed, Secretary of State George Shultz was able to argue convincingly that an arms race between us was absurd. We could not fight each other without committing suicide, and what rational leader was going to do that? In just a couple of years, we had abolished a whole class of nuclear weapons and our arsenals and, shortly thereafter, cut strategic nuclear weapons in half.

In concluding the New START agreement, which Ambassador McFaul has reminded us of, the Obama administration made an important contribution to our national security. But, since then, nuclear cooperation with Russia has deteriorated and seems practically nonexistent. It is urgent to restore that cooperation if we are to inhibit further proliferation. We are unlikely to do so if we proceed with plans to increase our military presence in Eastern Europe.

I am aware that one of our presumptive candidates for President has indicated that he might find some form of nuclear proliferation desirable. I believe that is profoundly mistaken, as is the idea that allies should pay us for their protection. I do not believe we should use our fine military as hired gendarmes to police the world, even if those protected were willing to pay the cost.

These comments, however, do reflect one important truth which we need to recognize, and that is that military alliances can create liabilities rather than augmenting power. When our interests are not closely aligned, an American security guarantee can create a moral hazard. What is to keep an "ally" from picking a fight unnecessarily and then expecting Uncle Sam to win it for him? Sounds like schoolyard bullying to me.

I have trouble, to take just one example today, to find much concurrence between American security interests and Turkish behavior. Is Turkey really an ally, or is it a problem? I don't want to single them out-I could use other examples.

Yes, when we have made commitments, we must honor them. But we must be more careful and selective about taking on liabilities. And some of our alliances formed under the different conditions of the Cold War should be reviewed. And I think that, increasingly, I believe you will find, if you question them, your constituents, many of them are worried about our over-military-involvement in the world, about attempts to use our fine military, the best in the world, to solve problems that can't be solved by military means and to carry out tasks that are more in the interests of other countries than they are in the United States.

We must set our priorities, and the highest priority should be the protection and security of the United States of America. The only thing that threatens our existence would be another nuclear arms race that gets out of hand.

Let's bear that in mind, because that is something President Ronald Reagan understood. Yes, he was a heavy critic of communism, but his idea was, yes, we have to stop the Soviet Union from expanding its influence; they have a crazy system. If that is what they want, that is their business. And, as a matter of fact, we didn't bring down communism; Gorbachev brought down communism. It was brought down by internal pressures, and it was brought down by internal pressures when we ended the Cold War and ended the external pressures on the Soviet Union. I think there are lessons here that we have sometimes forgotten.

Now, I have views on how we might deal with Russia on current issues such as Ukraine and Syria, democratization, and human rights and will share them if you wish. I believe there are

dignified ways we can reduce tensions with
Russia on those issues and others.

However, the main thing we should bear in mind,
that is, in confronting the greatest dangers to
civilized life in this country, such as terrorism-
didn't we have a reminder just 2 days ago in this
horrible massacre? Now, if there is any issue that
the U.S. and Russia have common interest, it is
in fighting terrorism. They are more vulnerable
than we are. Sometimes we tend to forget that.
And I still don't understand why we have not
been able to have more effective cooperation.

So I think the main thing we need to bear in mind
is that, in confronting these things, whether it be
terrorism, failed states, organized crime,
environmental degradation, U.S. and Russian
basic interests are not in conflict. As we deal
with them, as we must, Russia will either be part
of the problem or part of the solution. It is
obviously in our interest to do what we can to
encourage Russia to join us in confronting them.
They are unlikely to do so if they regard us as an
enemy or a competitor for influence in their
neighborhood.

As I said, we can argue about who is more
responsible for the situation, but the fact is that,
as you well know, politics is driven by

perceptions. And their perceptions are that we have been consistently moving against their interests and trying to encircle them and even trying to interfere in their internal politics.

Yes, President Putin has made many mistakes, many that are not in Russia's interests. But Russia's President, Russia's Government is a matter for Russians to decide. Their scandals are a matter for them to deal with. And I think when we presume--

Chairman ROYCE. Thank you, Professor Matlock.

Ambassador MATLOCK [continuing]. To do this ourselves, that is--

Chairman ROYCE. Thanks for--

Ambassador MATLOCK. Above all, I think we need to return to the position Reagan and Gorbachev set out: A nuclear war cannot be won, must never be fought, and that means there can be no war between us. To act on any other principle can create a risk to our Nation and the world of unimaginable gravity.

Chairman ROYCE. Thank you for those points.

We now go to Dr. Aron.

STATEMENT OF LEON ARON, PH.D., RESIDENT SCHOLAR AND DIRECTOR OF RUSSIAN STUDIES, THE AMERICAN ENTERPRISE INSTITUTE

Mr. ARON. Thank you very much, Mr. Chairman.

Mr. Chairman, Ranking Member, members of the committee, I don't have to remind anyone in this room that this is a tough, even rough, patch in the relations between the United States and Russia. There are many reasons for this troubling state of affairs, for which both sides bear responsibility.

But I would like to explore today one of the key elements of the present situation, and that is Vladimir Putin's system of beliefs, his vision of Russia in the world, and his understanding of his role as Russia's leader.

I want to do it because, contrary to a fairly popular view, I don't believe that his foreign policy, in particular his relationship with the United States, are made on an ad hoc basis. I think, instead, it is part of a long-term geopolitical project rooted deeply in his ideology, in his self-imposed personal historic mission, and

**36**

domestic political imperatives of his regime's survival.

There are few tenets in Vladimir Putin's credo that can be fairly ascertained now after his 16 years in power. Whether he was taking a break as the President or not, he was the effective leader. One, the end of the Cold War was Russia's equivalent of the 1919 Versailles Treaty for Germany, a source of endless humiliation and misery.

Two, the demise of the Soviet Union, in Putin's words, was "the greatest geopolitical tragedy of the 20th century."

Three, the overarching strategic agenda of a truly patriotic Russian leader, not an idiot or a traitor or both, as Putin almost certainly views Mikhail Gorbachev and Boris Yeltsin, is to recover and repossess for Russia political, economic, and geostrategic assets lost by the Soviet state at its fall. A few years back, I called this the Putin doctrine, and I think he has implemented it successfully and consistently virtually from day one of his Presidency.

In addition to his KGB training, these views are also shaped by Putin's favorite philosopher, Ivan Ilyin, whom the Russian President cites in speeches, assigns as reading to governors, and whose remains he had moved from Switzerland to re-inter on one of the most hollowed Russian grounds, the Donskoy Monastery in Moscow.

Ivan Ilyin believed, in essence, that Russia is never wrong but perennially wronged, primarily by the West; the West's hostility to Russia is eternal and prompted by the West's jealousy of Russia's size, natural riches, and, most of all, its incorruptible saintly soul and God-bestowed mission to be the third Rome, the light among nations; the plots against Russia are relentless, and, while truces are possible and often tactically advantageous to Russia, genuine peace with the West is very unlikely.

In addition to ideology-and Mike McFaul referred to this- Putin's foreign policy is also shaped by a large, I would say, urgent and powerful domestic political imperative. By the time of Putin's third Presidency, the toxic domestic economic climate had begun to reduce Russian economic growth to a crawl, even with the oil prices historically high. Most troubling for the regime, Putin's popularity, which was and continues to be a key to the regime's legitimacy, dropped by almost one-third between 2008 and 2011.

In the words of Putin's personal friend, trusted adviser, and former First Deputy Prime Minister and Minister of Finance, Alexei Kudrin, Russia had hit an institutional wall and needed a different economic model.

Putin chose to ignore this advice and reject it. And, instead of liberalizing institutional reforms, he made likely the most fateful decision of his political career: He began to shift the foundation of his regime's legitimacy from economic progress and steady growth of incomes to what might be called patriotic mobilization. There followed the annexation of Crimea, the hybrid war in Ukraine, and then Russia's involvement in Syria.

Putin appears to have stepped on an authoritarian escalator from which there is no exit except by physical demise or revolution. And the regime he is heading is presenting the West with an unprecedented challenge: A highly personalistic authoritarianism, which is resurgent, activist, inspired by a mission, prone to risky behavior both for ideological reasons and for those of domestic political legitimacy, and armed, by the latest count, with 1,735 strategic nuclear warheads on 521 delivery platforms.

Does that mean that the United States cannot

cooperate with Putin's Russia? Of course not, so long as we do not waste time and effort in areas where the gap in ultimate goals between Washington and Moscow is too wide to bridge, such as it is, I think, in Syria.

Yet there is one area where the coincidence of goals is not just possible but vital to the interests of the United States. Today, Russia does indeed find itself under siege-of course, not by the West, despite what the state propaganda machine asserts on national television daily. It is under the siege from what, in Mr. Rohrabacher's subcommittee a few months ago, I described as the Russian jihad. Russia is indeed under pressure domestically and from the outside. And I will be happy to provide you with the results of my research, but let me just mention that we can and should cooperate with Moscow in Central Asia. Central Asia is more vulnerable to Taliban and ISIS than any other region in the world today. Yes, it is primarily Russia's problem, yet it will be our problem, as well, when an area with a population of 68 million people becomes a terrorist haven and a magnet for would-be world jihadists.

Mr. Chairman, in conclusion, I would like to ask that a recent article of mine in Foreign Policy titled "Playing Tic-Tac-Toe with Putin" is entered into the record.

Thank you very much.

Chairman ROYCE. Without objection. Very good. We will enter that into the record, Dr. Aron.

I was going to ask you about your perceptions on Central Asia and where we could cooperate here. And I think your point about recruitment-there are literally thousands of recruits coming out of Russia into ISIS right now, but, on top of that, there is the wider problem of this radicalization and the pace of it.

It seems to me that there is this room for cooperation, but, at the same time, there are questions about what Putin would seek from us, what could he offer. There is also the question in terms of associating ourselves with Putin's counterterrorism efforts, because I am not sure what form they would take, given the way in which we try to conduct our counterterrorism operations with a great deal of, shall we say, care.

And what is, obviously, most vexing to me is watching Syria. Instead of hitting ISIS, he hit the Free Syrian Army, and instead of hitting the army, he hit the markets. His bombers hit, you

know, the hospitals, hit the schools. This aspect
of this is what is so troublesome for us in the
West because it seems counterproductive in
terms of the effort of actually going after Islamist
terrorism. So walk us through how, Dr. Aron, we
could engage on that front.

Mr. ARON. Well, on Syria, I mentioned, yes, all
those things you mentioned could be summarized
under the heading of "Different, Divergent
Goals." The goal of Putin in Syria is (A) to save
the Assad regime, and we could discuss why he
wants it; (B) to present the West with a total
repugnant choice between Assad and ISIS; and
(C) have Russia as the dominant outside player in
the Middle East. Clearly, neither of those is our
goal.

In Central Asia, on the other hand, I think the
goals do coincide. Let me remind you, Mr.
Chairman, last week there was not just a terrorist
act, there was street fighting in the city of Aktobe
in Kazakhstan between government troops and
terrorists. That is 400 kilometers from Russia's
borders. You know, that is less than 250 miles.

Churchill was mentioned here, I think by Jack
Matlock. Central Asia is the soft underbelly of
Russia. This is an enormous area. You know that
there are 6 million guest workers, many of them

illegal, in Russia coming in and out from Central Asia. Russia is the major recruitment center for ISIS, an estimated 300 to 500 recruiters. Most of Central Asians have been recruited not in Kazakhstan or Tajikistan or Kyrgyzstan, they were recruited on construction sites in Moscow to join ISIS.

There are all kinds of statistics. For example, Russian speakers from Russia and the former Soviet Union, primarily Central Asia, are the second-largest language group in ISIS after Arabic speakers.

We cannot help Putin inside the country, and we could discuss why he has this problem inside the country-radicalization of its own Muslims and the guest workers. But in Central Asia, I believe, Tajikistan, Kyrgyzstan, and, to a certain extent, Uzbekistan and Kazakhstan are very troubled states. If they fall, as I said, the danger to us is that they will become havens for terrorists.

Chairman ROYCE. But let me just add a point, because Mr. Engeland I have traveled in Central Asia, and we have had many meetings and many explanations from local government officials about how Gulf-state money floods into that region and acquires either radio stations, television stations, newspapers; increasingly,

how also imams come from another part of the
world--

Mr. ARON. Right.

Chairman ROYCE [continuing]. And change the
indigenous Muslim faith, or ideology, to a new
ideology. As they would say to us, these are not
our customs, these are customs that are being
imported here, but they are changing our culture.

And it looks like what we see happening across
Central Asia is also happening across southern
Russia. And that, then, leads to this problem. And
I would argue this is going to be the next big
problem because of the rate at which this is
happening.

The last point I wanted to ask you-I am almost
out of time- is just some of the stuff that we hear
on RT television or in Russian propaganda-the
Zika virus was created by the United States. You
know, you have a $450 million budget spreading
this kind of nonsense across Latin America,
Central Asia, Europe, around the world, here, a
lot of disinformation, 24 hours a day.

There has to be a more effective way to move
forward to counter this disinformation, get the
facts out there, and, item by item, knock this stuff

down, you know, knock this narrative down with the truth about what is going on, because, obviously, it is having an impact among the Russian-speaking population in Eastern Europe, certainly, but beyond that now. This is being translated in all these other languages. And it is just a constant, big lie, propaganda effort that has to be countered.

Dr. Aron, any response on that?

Mr. ARON. Well, Mr. Chairman, I have to put on my BBG Governor hat. We have a good relationship with your committee. We are working together to make U.S. international broadcasting more effective.

Let me tell you, though, that my own experience is that, ultimately, the most effective countermeasure to the Russian propaganda is not just the U.S. airwaves but empowering the local Russian-speaking population in former Soviet Union.

Chairman ROYCE. Reporters and stringers?

Mr. ARON. Reporters, stringers--

Chairman ROYCE. Uh-huh.

Mr. ARON [continuing]. Through nongovernment and government grants.

One of the examples that I believe I gave, testifying on the issue of the Russian propaganda in the Senate, was StopFake, which is a very effective site in Kiev run by the students of the department of journalism of the Mohyla Academy.

This is ultimately the only way to counter the Russian propaganda, because it gives the people of those countries-and, of course, this could be spread. Similar efforts are occurring in the Baltics and in Central Asia.

Chairman ROYCE. Thank you, Dr. Aron.

Mr. Eliot Engel of New York.

Mr. ENGEL. Thank you, Mr. Chairman.

Ambassador McFaul, I wanted to discuss with you a little bit about one of the things you mentioned when you said that Ukraine is central to blocking Putin.

I have been really at odds with U.S. policy toward Ukraine. First of all, back in 2008, I think it was a strategic blunder that NATO did not admit Ukraine-and Georgia, by the way-in 2008. I know that the Bush administration said that they pushed to have it done but that the Germans and then, to a lesser degree, the French blocked it. I think that Putin's aggression in both those countries would not have happened if they had been members of NATO. I think our lack of bringing them into NATO makes it virtually impossible for them to come into NATO in the future, and I think that was a time lost.

I think that Ukraine is so important. It is really the center of where we have our disagreements with Russia. If we allow Crimea to just be annexed and do nothing about it, don't even talk about it anymore, if we allow Putin to start this nonsense in-if we allow Putin to continue his nonsense, I should say-in eastern Ukraine- you know, reports indicate that the fighting has stepped up again in Ukraine. And it seems that every time Putin feels pressure in one part of the world he will intensify the military campaign in the Ukrainian east as a valve to release that pressure. And, you know, at the same time, Ukraine is fighting serious corruption problems, and it limits its government's ability to respond to the Russian aggression.

I mean, I just think that we have the most pro-Western government in Ukraine that we could possibly have, and God forbid that government falls. It will be 100 years before we will have anything like that.

And, to me, this really strikes at the core of NATO. If we want NATO to continue to be successful and not just worthless, it seems to me Ukraine is where we make our stand.

I disagree with the administration's lack of providing weapons to the people of Ukraine. I know they feel that Ukraine can never beat Russia, and so, if we provide Ukraine with more weapons, it will just escalate the situation. But I think Putin makes a different calculation. When Russian soldiers start coming home in body bags, I think that his calculation will be different, that he can just make trouble whenever he wants to and there will be no price to pay.

So I want you to expand on Ukraine, because I think that is really where it is all about. And shame on us if we allow that regime in Ukraine to falter.

Ambassador MCFAUL. Thank you for the question. I agree. I agree with everything you just said. I do believe that the best way to support reform and those that care about democracy and markets in Russia is to have Ukraine succeed. I believe that the best way to deter further aggression from Ukraine is to help Ukraine succeed. It is when the government is collapsing, when democracy is not working, when the economy is not producing that creates the permissive conditions for more mischief. So I really do think the key moment in all of European security right now is what this government will do over the next 2 to 10 years. This is a long-haul issue. This is not something that is going to be solved in 6 months.

Mr. ENGEL. "This government" meaning which government? Ambassador MCFAUL. The Ukrainian Government.

Mr. ENGEL. The Ukrainian Government. Ambassador MCFAUL. Yes.

Now, I would disagree slightly. I think there were people that used to be in the government that were better. You know, Minister Jaresko, for instance, was, I think, a great Finance Minister, the former Minister of the Economy. I hope to see them back again. But, generally, I think the glass is half-full, not half-empty. They are doing some extraordinary things, especially on the macroeconomic front, when facing some real big challenges. And, you know, talking to some very senior folks over at the IMF in the last few days, they are pleased with the progress they have made. The one issue that they agree, that the Ukrainians agree, and I agree that needs more focus is a fight against corruption and to get the oligarchs out of the political process. That is going to be a long process, and we should be engaged in that process. I think what happens in Ukraine really determines the fate of what Russia will do with respect to that part of the world.

With respect to Europe, with NATO, I would just say two things. One, I disagree-I want to make sure everybody understands I do disagree with Ambassador Matlock right now. Whether it was right to expand NATO or not, we could relitigate that. We were probably on different sides of that debate. But to pull back now, I think, would be a very dangerous thing because it would create a vacuum, it would create uncertainty about our commitment to our NATO allies.

And, to me, the best way to keep the peace-we are all quoting Ronald Reagan. Let me quote one more Ronald Reagan quote. I am also at the Hoover Institution, by the way. "Peace through strength." So Putin needs to have zero doubt in his mind that we are going to have our Article 5 commitments to our allies, including our allies the Baltic states and Poland. And that is why I support making that clear.

By the time when we got to the government, just to be clear about the historical record, the debate about Ukraine joining NATO was over. Whether that was good or bad, again, we can talk about that; it was not on the agenda. So when I see on RT that they are doing this in Crimea to stop NATO expansion, it is nonsense. There was no NATO expansion.

I was in the government for 5 years, and pretty much every meeting with Mr. Putin and Mr. Medvedev and on every phone call but one, the issue of NATO expansion never came up once, because the issue was over. Ukraine was not asking to join NATO. NATO did not want Ukraine to join. After the election in 2010, Mr. Yanukovych even more so did not.

It all is a post facto rationalization for what Putin did in Ukraine that he brings that up. And I think we need to be clear about that historical record.

Mr. ENGEL. Okay. Thank you.

Ambassador MCFAUL. Thank you.

Mr. ENGEL. Thank you.

Chairman ROYCE. Thank you.

We go to Mr. Dana Rohrabacher of California.

Mr. ROHRABACHER. Yes. And thank you very much, Mr. Chairman, for making sure that this was a very balanced hearing today. And I appreciate that, realizing that some of the things that I believe are going on in the policies here don't reflect very many of my fellow members' ideas of what the policies should be. But we are all trying to be honest and trying to make a better world, trying to find a way that we can actually have peace between two of these major countries, the United States and Russia.

And I am proud to have played a role in Ronald Reagan's efforts to defeat communism and end the Cold War and, yes, Ronald Reagan's intent to create a new era of friendship between the United States, the people of the United States, and the people of Russia. And I know that Ambassador Matlock played an important role in this, as well, and I am very happy to see him and hear him with us today.

Let me just note, I have been watching this for a long time, as well, and I am appalled at the depth that we have let our relationship sink to at this point. We are at the lowest point of any time since the ending of the Cold War.

And I do not believe, as some people have indicated already that they believe, that all of this can be related to Putin. The fact is there has been an unrelenting hostility toward Russia from the very days that we were negotiating with them and they were making concessions that led to tearing down the Berlin Wall; that led to the withdrawal of Soviet troops, which were no longer Soviet troops, were Russian troops from Eastern Europe; which led to major arms reduction agreements between our countries; that, even during those times, there was an element that hated Russia. Over and over again, we would hear it. And some of them had very good reasons, because their family were murdered by communists, who happened to be Russians, during the Cold War.

And also we had people who just could not get over the fact that it was not Russia that was the enemy in the Cold War, it wasn't the Russian people, but was, indeed, communism that was the enemy. It was the communism that spurred Russia to build these rockets and missiles that threatened us, to support radical elements around the world, to create revolutions in order to establish atheistic communist dictatorships throughout the world. That was communism. That wasn't the Russian people.

But yet there have been thousands of documents that have just recently been declassified-Mr. Matlock, I want to ask you if you have seen some of these and whether you agree with them-that did say that we actually proposed to the Russians that, if they would withdraw their troops from Eastern Europe, that at that point we would not be expanding NATO, and we gave them the impression they would be integrated into the economies of Western Europe and the world. And, in either case, there was no ability for the Russians to get into Europe. That is not even a question. But, at the same time, we end up expanding NATO.

Was there an understanding, although it wasn't written down, that we would not have an expansion of NATO, so that Russians would withdraw their troops and troops with guns aimed at Russia would not go right up to their border? Was that an understanding at that time, Mr. Matlock?

Ambassador MATLOCK. It was indeed. It was indeed the understanding at that time. Now, this was not a legal commitment. Mr. ROHRABACHER. Right.

Ambassador MATLOCK. I must say I testified in the Senate against the original NATO expansion because I thought it was not in the U.S. interest, and I thought it was not necessary to begin to divide Europe again. At the end of the Cold War, we had a Europe whole and free, and that was the objection. You don't keep a Europe whole and free by taking what had been a Cold War alliance, which should have been preserved as it was, and using it by moving the things left, and it was quite predictable then that if we did.

So the reason that I had for not expanding NATO was the interest of the United States. However, it is quite true that the Bush administration and our allies, particularly our Germans, made statements during German unification that clearly implied that if the Soviet Union did not use force in Eastern Europe, and allow Germany to allow and stay in NATO, there would be no expansion of NATO jurisdiction.

Mr. ROHRABACHER. And this--

Ambassador MATLOCK. At one point, Secretary Baker said not one inch to the east, and Gorbachev answered that, of course, that would be unacceptable. They were talking about east Germany, but the language is general.

Mr. ROHRABACHER. Mr. Chairman--

Ambassador MATLOCK. That was the understanding. Now, it was not a legal question.

Mr. ROHRABACHER. Let me jump in here for a moment. That was long before there was ever any Mr. Putin, and in fact, this is long before any of these "hostile acts" that we are being told about happened. That was an indication of what? That people were still going to be treating Russia as if it was the Soviet Union. And so right from the beginning, we have had this incredible hostility that-and just let me note, we have, for example, buzzing our airplanes right now, buzzing-are being buzzed by Russian airplanes, our ships. The American people see that.

Well, where are our ships? The ship that was being buzzed-I don't remember where I heard this-was in the Baltic Sea and here it was, I don't know how many miles from St. Petersburg, but why are we sending our U.S. military forces that close to Russia? We have nuclear weapons delivery systems that are being aimed at Russia. How else would they think of that except as being a hostile act? And for them to buzz a ship to see what kind of ship it was right off their borders.

By the way, some of these ships that we have sent there are closer to Russia than Catalina

Island is to Los Angeles. What if some nuclear weapons delivery system showed up there? What would we think? Would we send an airplane out to buzz it around and see what kind of ship it is?

I think that both sides, both Russia and the United States need to take a deep breath and step back from this whole military operation that are actually making things worse rather than making things better, and we need to find out where our differences are, negotiate them, see where we can work together.

And Mr. Aron, thank you very much for your wonderful testimony today, which is aimed at where we need to work together, or we are all going to suffer because radical Islam is the threat today, not the Soviet Union. And so, I appreciate you focusing on where we could cooperate, which would be better for both of us. So thank you, Mr. Chairman, and--

Chairman ROYCE. Thank you, Mr. Rohrabacher.

Mr. ROHRABACHER. I will be ready for a second round if we have it.

Chairman ROYCE. Okay. And we are going to go to Mr. Gregory Meeks of New York.

Mr. MEEKS. Thank you, Mr. Chairman.

Let me first say, Ambassador McFaul, you are right, and that I have learned a lot listening to all three of you. As you said in your initial statements, it has been very--

Ambassador MCFAUL. And I will send you my book for free, okay.

Mr. MEEKS. Okay. I will take it. I will read it. I have a long trip. It will be good to read. And let me also say that, for me, you know, I consider myself a multilateralist, and I believe that diplomacy is the best way to try to resolve things. And you know, I have heard the conversations going back and forth about President Reagan and Gorbachev. Well, we can always go back to Kennedy and Khrushchev. Even when we were at the height of this danger of nuclear weapons, the dialogue between them continued. In fact, President Kennedy also went to the Soviet Union then to meet with Khrushchev so that they could have conversations, and there were telephone calls going back and forth in trying to make sure that we didn't have a major catastrophic scenario that could have ruined the world actually.

And so, for me, to cast off and say that we shouldn't talk to one country or another just does not make sense in this day and age. It didn't make sense in the 1960s, and it still doesn't make sense today in 2016. And so we have to figure out, in my estimation, on how do we do talk and work with one another. And when I initially came into Congress, with me, there were two huge countries that are important. Sometimes we get along with them and sometimes we don't, but we have got to figure this out.

Russia is one of them. Turkey is the other. Because when you talk about the global context, you can't act as though they don't exist because they do. And so much so, that I was, at that time, tried to establish and we were moving a long a Russian caucus. We would talk with the Russians on a regular basis and try to get to know members of their Parliament, because sometimes I think when you have parliamentarian-to-parliamentarian conversation relationships, that helps things, as opposed to breaking things down, and I, for one, think that that is a direction that we still need to move in, and I think it is tremendously important. And as you said, Ambassador McFaul, in this current administration, there is a lot that we have done together, a lot of things. Some, you know, when you talk about the START Treaty and the interest of WTO, security, U.N. Security Council, dealing with, you know, the sanctions against Iran as far as nuclear weapons are concerned because it is all in our mutual interest, and I agree with you 100 percent in regards to supporting and making sure we are there for our NATO allies and not pulling out.

Now, it seems to me, and I just want to be corrected one way or the other, that when Medvedev was in charge, there was really close dialogue, et cetera. Now, some will tell me that Putin was always in charge, and he was the guy in the background. And so when it ended, and Putin came back in, it seemed to me that there then became some real problems with reference to communication, even with reference to you as Ambassador to Russia, and whether or not the reset agreement, whether or not that was successful or not.

Can you tell me what happened? Why, you know, in that change, especially when Putin was in charge all along, what happened right in that period so that our relationships at least try to work in a common interest on things that are common to both of us, what happened in that time?

Ambassador MCFAUL. So Congressman, thank you for that great question that I can't do justice to in a minute-and-a-half, but I think it is a fundamental question, because if we don't get the answer right, the prescriptions are going to be wrong.

I just want to remind you that we did have this period of cooperation, and your efforts, Congressman, I just want to applaud. I think engagement is always good. Even if you disagree, you want to know why you are disagreeing, and somebody-we were talking earlier about cooperation on counterintelligence with terrorists. We did that, Mr. Chairman. We did that with the Russians. And you remember, you and I spent a really interesting day down at the KGB offices, right, learning in terms of cooperation. We were doing all those things.

Moreover, I just want to read you-you don't have to believe. Let me quote President Medvedev speaking about NATO at the NATO summit in Lisbon. I was there with him. This is what he said on the record, and I will tell you what he said after the record later. He said, "Incidentally"-this is the President of Russia-"even a declaration approved at the end of our talks states that we seek to develop a strategic partnership. This is not a chance choice of words, but signals that we have succeeded in putting the difficult period in our relations behind us now."

That is the President of Russia. That is not Barack Obama. That is the President of Russia just a few years ago, so you have to explain what happened after that--

Mr. MEEKS. That is right.

Ambassador MCFAUL [continuing]. To understand the conflict. And in my view, just to re-underscore it, it has to do with Putin coming back. Yes, he was the grand decision maker all the time. We dealt with both the Prime Minister and the President when I was in the government, but at the end of day, he had a much more suspicious view of the United States, and in particular, a suspicious view that we go around the world overthrowing regimes, either covertly or overtly that we don't like.

And by way, there is a lot of data to support his hypothesis about American foreign policy over the last 70 years. And so the President-I was at many of these meetings, and the President would sit with Putin and say, The CIA is not supporting the overthrow of Mubarak. The CIA is not supporting the overthrow of your regime. These Russians, some of them are in the back here actually, they are actually acting on their own. These Ukrainians, they are actually acting on their own. They are not controlled by the United

**62**

States of America.

Putin didn't want to believe that. Now, whether he knew the truth but didn't want to believe it for political purposes or genuinely didn't believe it- we used to argue about that in the administration, but he decided that he needed us as an enemy, to discredit these people.

And the last thing. We have heard-and you know, there is blame to go around, and I am happy to talk about some of the mistakes that we made if I had more time, because I do think we made a few mistakes in the Obama administration. But I want to radically reject this moral equivalency that somehow we are all to blame here, and you know, that it is blame on America, blame on the United States. I want to know precisely what the Obama administration did to cause this conflict, because I can tell you precisely what Putin did.

If we had the 10 Commandments about how to be a good multilateralist, how to be a good international citizen, at the top three, one of them would be: Thou shall not annex the territory of thy neighbor.

And I am sorry, that is what he did.

Mr. MEEKS. That is right.

Ambassador MCFAUL. We didn't annex any territory. We didn't support any revolution against him, and there has to be a response to that. We just can't sit on our hands and say, Well, you know, let's all try to get along here. No, there has to be a response. Thou does not-especially in Europe, we cannot allow annexation to become policy that does not have a response.

Having said all that, I want to remind you that even during the conflict that we had, we still managed to cooperate with Mr. Putin. I was there with him when we did the chemical weapons deal between the United States and Russia in September 2003. That is smart diplomacy. We managed the P5+1 negotiations on Iran, even during this time, and some of these other issues, including terrorism, if we can cooperate where it is in our national interest, we should, but we have to also respond to these aggressive things when they happen.

Mr. MEEKS. Absolutely.

Chairman ROYCE. We are going to go to Mr. Steve Chabot of Ohio.

Mr. CHABOT. Thank you, Mr. Chairman.

Ambassador MATLOCK. Since I was mentioned,

**64**

may I make a statement here. I have never used moral equivalency. This is not my--

Ambassador MCFAUL. I did not--

Ambassador MATLOCK. Nor have I ever--

Ambassador MCFAUL. I didn't mention you, Jack.

Ambassador MATLOCK. You did.

Ambassador MCFAUL. I didn't mean to.

Chairman ROYCE. If I could--

Ambassador MCFAUL. I was quoting my own testimony.

Chairman ROYCE. If I could go to Mr. Steve Chabot of Ohio, he has some questions.

Mr. CHABOT. Thanks. I have just have a couple of points first before I ask any question. I think it is pretty clear to me and a number of us that I think this administration's withdrawal from America's traditional leadership role has left a power vacuum around the globe, one that Putin has taken advantage of, as well as other bad actors. ISIS, obviously, comes to mind, China building islands in the South China Sea, and then militarizing them.

But Putin, with invading Crimea, and to a great extent, I think the West lamely protested, but ultimately did little or nothing, I would like to commend my colleague from the Commonwealth of Virginia for his attention on Crimea, for example, and my colleague, the ranking member, obviously has stressed in his remarks of Crimea that we not forget what has happened there, because I think the world has to a great extent.

But you know, after basically invading and then having a bogus referendum and essentially taken over the country, they have continued with aggression in eastern Ukraine, and the Ukraines have fought bravely, but they are just outgunned. Putin has also been expanding Russia's military footprint in places like Armenia, which has welcomed thousands of Russian troops and an infusion of advanced weaponry, and this has resulted in Putin pressuring NATO's southern flank, just as the alliance is trying to reinforce its eastern flank, and having been to Poland and Latvia and Lithuania and Estonia and Hungary and other countries in the region, a lot of these countries are just scared to death with what Putin is up to.

But Putin continues to hone in on Nagorno-
Karabakh, an area that we don't talk about that
much anymore. We talked about it maybe a
couple of decades back, but not much anymore,
but it is a region that is vulnerable to conflict,
and tensions have flared up and deaths are
occurring there. There has been military action
there in recent months, and I believe he hopes
this arrangement, Nagorno-Karabakh will shore
up his international reputation and pull Armenia
and Azerbaijan closer to Russia and further away
from the West.

Putin's engagement in Syria in the Middle East
has only complicated matters there. As the U.S.
works to defeat a ruthless terrorist group, ISIS in
the region, Putin undermines our efforts, to a
great extent, by lending support to the Assad
regime, continuing to test the limits of Turkey,
supplying weapons systems to Iran, and on and
on.

But let me-and I don't have a huge amount of
time, obviously, even less. Let me go to the first
point that I raised about Crimea. I think that, you
know, the world, unfortunately, to a considerable
degree, has accepted this as a fait accompli. You
don't hear much in the news about it about-in the
press much at all. It is my understanding that the
repression there is worsening, that Russia is

tightening its grip on Crimea, that they are escalating their campaign against dissents, and Dr. Aron, would you comment on what is happening in Crimea and what the rest of the world ought to be doing about it, including the United States now?

Mr. ARON. Well, thank you very much, and I am sure my colleagues could comment, too. Just the latest number by the refugee agency, Ukrainian refugee agency, but I think they are being quite honest here. About 100,000 refugees left Crimea. Now, this is out of a population of probably half a million. What I find most dangerous--

Mr. CHABOT. That is 20 percent of the population has left their country?

Mr. ARON. Approximately. Approximately. I mean, you know, these numbers, because nobody could get there without being harassed, and many are barred from going there, many international organizations by Russia, it is hard to say, but the numbers are staggering.

What concerns me-and I would like to circle back to my issue of the Russian jihad, is that as far as we could establish, in percentage terms, relative to their population, the greatest ethnic representation in ISIS is Crimean Tatars, at

**68**

between 300 and 500 people, and there are no more than 120,000 Crimea Tatars. Now, this is greatly exacerbated by the fact that Putin dissolved the selfgoverning body of the Crimea Tatars in Crimea. He prevented their leaders, including Mosad Jamilif, former Soviet dissident, from coming back to their homeland, returning.

So there is a whole group of exiles now in Ukraine. So this all exacerbates the situation, and it, again, feeds into extremism in the case of Crimean Tatars. Because when I spoke about the danger of the Russian jihad, from the inside, the key danger is that the Islamic militancy that used to be confined largely to North Caucasus is now spreading inside Russia. It is spreading toward Tatarstan. It is spreading toward the fringes. Of course, always the fringes, of about 6 million strong Central Asian Diaspora in Russia. So Crimea, in addition to being a gross violation of international norms, in addition to being a gross violation of human rights of the Crimean Tatars and others who live in Crimea, it is also a very dangerous situation where it could lead to the rise of Islamic extremism.

Mr. CHABOT. Thank you.

Mr. ROHRABACHER [presiding]. Thank you very much, Dr. Aron, and-thank you, and look who has got the gavel now.

Ms. BASS. Oh, oh, we are all in trouble.

Mr. ROHRABACHER. My goodness, isn't democracy wonderful.

I now recognize Karen Bass. Thank you very much.

Ms. BASS. Why, thank you, Mr. Chair.

One, I just wanted to thank the panelists. I really appreciated all the testimony, and I wanted to agree with my colleague here, Representative Meeks, that I am sure all of us learned a lot from what each of you had to say.

I wanted to ask, Ambassador Matlock, you referred to, in your testimony, that you had some additional views on how we could reduce tension. You also said that-I believe you said that one thing that we shouldn't do is increase our military involvement, or require payments from NATO countries, and then you cautioned on taking on liabilities.

And I was wondering, the ranking member is talking about legislation that would impose additional sanctions, and I wondered about your comments within that context, and if we did impose additional sanctions, would that be an example of the liabilities that you were concerned about?

Ambassador MATLOCK. Yes. Thank you very much for the question. Obviously, in just a few minutes, I cannot go into great detail. Let me first address the issue of Ukraine in Crimea.

I think everything said by the others has been correct, but they have taken a lot of things out of context. And frankly, I do not agree that our new national security is significantly affected by what happens in Ukraine. I think we have to have certain priorities. And second, I am certain there is no way to solve the problem militarily. Let's look at reality. Russia, given its history, given its close association, is not going to allow the Ukrainian situation to be solved militarily, so giving military aid, encouraging a military response simply causes more damage to the area, and it is not going to be solved that way.

The basic thing we have to bear in mind, and this is unfortunate, but it is reality, and that is, you cannot have a united prosperous Ukraine which does not have close relations with Russia. And the second thing is, if you look at the politics and history and the economics, Ukraine is better off without Crimea. Now, I don't like the way Russians took it, and we should not recognize it, as we don't. However, to think that by bringing pressure to bear on them we can make them change their policy simply plays into Putin's hands because it makes it a national issue. So any attempts to use military force or to encourage it will make the situation worse.

Now, that is one thing. Now, on the-this is true of some of these other issues. Obviously, terrorism is a threat to both of us. I think that we need to define our aims as to what the ultimate aim is. Our aim in Syria should not be to remove the leader, whoever he is. Our aim should be to do what we can to keep the country from falling apart to keep ISIS out, to keep the refugees out of Europe. Now, the Russian opinion has been, you will get more chaos in Syria if you remove the current regime the way we did in Iraq, the way we did in Libya. They have a point. Can't we understand that? Ms. BASS. Can I ask you, if the ranking--

Ambassador MATLOCK. I think what we need to do is to concentrate on those areas where our interests are and find better ways to do them.

Ms. BASS. Thank you.

Ambassador MATLOCK. As far as Russia's internal government, Russians are going to decide that. And to the degree that we try to interfere, they look at it just as we looked at the Communist Party during the Cold War.

Ms. BASS. Okay.

Ambassador MATLOCK. That is if our democratization efforts are simply in opposition to the current regime. They are going to react to that.

Ms. BASS. Let me ask, Ambassador McFaul, I wanted to one question. And thank you very much, Ambassador Matlock. What do you see as the future? I mean, do you think that Putin is going to make a switch again? I don't know when his "term" is over, but do you think that he will switch again and become the Prime Minister and prop up another President? What is your best guess?

Ambassador MCFAUL. So first of all, I just want to be clear about this. To the degree that which we interfere, Putin is going to react. I totally agree with Ambassador Matlock on that. What I disagree is the assumption that somehow we are interfering.

We did not give one penny to the democratic opposition when I was in the U.S. Government, and I just want to make that clear because I think you said "perceptions." Well, perceptions have to be rebutted when they are not true, okay. We are not fomenting revolution in Russia and--

Ambassador MATLOCK. But they had an Assistant Secretary of State speaking on a telephone, cell phone that could be monitored talking about who should be the Prime Minister of Ukraine in a revolutionary situation.

Ambassador MCFAUL. I was speaking on--

Ambassador MATLOCK. Now, what are the Russians going to think about that?

Ambassador MCFAUL. Well, that was a mistake. I agree with you. Ambassador MATLOCK. Not only was it a mistake, it was--

Ambassador MCFAUL. It was a mistake, but if you want to know the full details, it was the mistake in the--

Ambassador MATLOCK. And you wonder about perceptions.

Ambassador MCFAUL. Well, let me give you

the--

Ambassador MATLOCK. If it had happened in--

Ambassador MCFAUL. Doctor--

Ambassador MATLOCK [continuing]. Cuba or Mexico, how would we have reacted?

Ambassador MCFAUL. So let me give you the full context of that conversation if you are interested. The conversation was about how to get a coalition government together with President Yanukovych. We, the United States Government, the Obama administration, were seeking to diffuse tensions on the streets, and we, on February 21, worked hard with our European allies to cut a deal between the opposition and Mr. Yanukovych, President Yanukovych. The Vice President called him about a dozen times to cut a deal between him and the street. We were not trying to overthrow Mr. Yanukovych, and 12 hours later, for some unexpected reason, he showed up in Rostov. To this day, I don't know why he fled. So--

Ms. BASS. My question--

Ambassador MCFAUL [continuing]. You said we need context-- Ms. BASS [continuing]. About

Putin--

Ambassador MCFAUL. There is little context.

Ms. BASS. Hello.

Ambassador MCFAUL. But I want to come back
to your question, Ma'am.

Ms. BASS. Thank you.

Ambassador MCFAUL. I am a giant optimist
about Russia. I want to make that clear. I am a
huge optimist about Russia. I can't predict when
and where, and the interregnum, I have no
prediction about, but I, as a social scientist, I
study political and economic change around the
world, and Russia is a rich country. Russia has a
rising middle class. Most Russians want to be
integrated into the world, and yes, Russians
should be in charge of their own fate. But
Russians, all of them, not just Mr. Putin or that
regime, and I just don't think those structural
forces of change that Russia is going to somehow
be the one country that becomes middle income
or high-when they become an even higher
income country, and be the one country that will
not move in this kind of forces for political and
economic modernization.

I just have met too many young people that are just like my students at Stanford that just want a normal life. They want a good job, they want to travel abroad, and they want their government to represent them--

Mr. ROHRABACHER [presiding]. Thank you.

Ambassador MCFAUL. And so in the long run, I am incredibly optimistic about Russia. I just don't know how long the long run is.

Mr. ROHRABACHER. Thank you, Mr. Ambassador.

Mr. ARON. Chairman Rohrabacher--

Mr. ROHRABACHER. The Chair will recognize Mr. Joe Wilson of South Carolina.

Mr. WILSON. Thank you, Acting Chairman Dana Rohrabacher. And it is right on point. I have been optimistic about a U.S./Russian friendship. And I have had a number of visits have been very inspiring to me to promote nuclear cooperation, building friendships with the people of Russia from Moscow to St. Petersburg to Novosibirsk and Siberia. I have been very grateful that my home community of Columbia is the sister city of Shiabinsk. I have had wonderful visits. And every time I go, I have been so impressed by the people of Russia, the culture of Russia.

I have had members of the Duma visit our office. They have been welcomed. But sadly, things have not developed like I anticipated. Additionally, in my home community of South Carolina, the midlands of South Carolina, we welcomed a large number of very prosperous Russian Americans to our community. In fact, the Columbia Civic Ballet could be misidentified as the St. Petersburg Civic Ballet, and we welcome the-again, the extraordinary contributions of Russian Americans to our State.

But sadly, the high hopes that I had of mutual benefit cooperation, as you indicated, with growing middle class travel has really been crushed by the aggression that I have personally seen in our extraordinarily brave ally, the Republic of Georgia, and that hasn't been mentioned. That was 2008. And then, of course, the aggression in Ukraine.

With that, Dr. Aron, in April 2016, Russian fighter jets flew within 30 feet of the USS Donald Cook, then flew a Russian interceptor within 50 feet of American reconnaissance aircraft. Could you explain the rationale between such bizarrely dangerous actions on the part of Russia and what can be done by the United States and our allies to curtail such activity?

Mr. ARON. My goodness, that is quite a question. Before I answer, just a factual correction, if I may. I misspoke. The population of Crimea is 2 million people. So 100,000 refugees constitutes about 5 percent, not 20 percent, an important correction.

I am a big believer, and I know-and I know Jack Matlock may not agree with that, but I think Mike McFaul, and I think similarly about these things. I think most of these acts are done for domestic political purposes. The government of 3 years ago, before Ukraine, before anything else, a top Russian political sociologist, whose name I will not mention, just I don't want to get him in trouble, told me, Leon, you know, why are you talking about foreign policy as something separate from domestic? The only thing going for this regime is its foreign policy. This is where the legitimacy is. Russia rising off its knees again, Russia is where the Soviet Union used to be, and Vladimir Putin secured Russia as a great super power again.

We underestimated the appeal that this caused in the hearts and minds of millions of Russians because we underestimated the hurt that occurred when the Soviet Union collapsed. So these singular facts of bringing it to the brink and bringing it to the point is to show domestically that Putin is not intimidated by the United States, that he is ready to take all the necessary means to defend Russia against the danger that may not exist.

I think Mike McFaul and I agree on this. The point is that he is almost forced to act provocatively because that is where his regime support and legitimacy and popularity is.

Mr. WILSON. And, but again, 30 feet, 50 feet, that is ridiculous. The obvious extraordinary loss of life that could occur is so irresponsible, and not in the interest of the people of Russia, or its foreign policy or its military.

Mr. ARON. Sir, as I said in the concluding remarks to my statement, we are facing an unprecedented danger, a risk-prone, highly personalistic authoritarian regime that acts both out of mission and out of ideology. It is pushed toward these types of acts, and that is what scares me the most.

Mr. WILSON. You mentioned Foreign Affairs magazine, and yesterday, General Philip

Breedlove, the former commander of European commander and NATO supreme allied commander, had an article that I am confident you probably already read, that America needs to do more to deter the Russian threat. And so I, again, appreciate all of your service, and I thank you very much for being here today. And I yield back to the--

Mr. ARON. Thank you.

Mr. WILSON [continuing]. Acting chairman, of all people, Dana Rohrabacher.

Mr. ROHRABACHER. Well, thank you. Now, let me get this straight. You have a candidate somewhere saying he wants to make his country great again? And then takes over the reigns of power? That could never happen really in a modern society, could it?

All right. It is supposed to be a joke. That was supposed to be funny. All right. We now have Mr. Boyle.

Mr. BOYLE. Thank you, and thank you to all three of the witnesses. I have several things I want to go over, but first, I can't help the irony that we are having this hearing, and literally, in the last 5 minutes, The Washington Post is reporting that according to security experts, Russian Government hackers have hacked the Democratic National Committee to find oppo research that the DNC has, and that is according to our own security experts. So spare me the moral equivalency language that mistakes have been made on both sides.

Second point I would like to make is I know that there are some who want to conveniently take shots at President Obama and the Obama administration over what happened in Crimea, and that somehow if the U.S. President had been stronger, this would have been prevented. Is it Hungary, 1956, President Eisenhower; 1968, Czechoslovakia would have been Lyndon Johnson; 2008, when George W. Bush was President, the invasion of Georgia. Those were previous Presidents, both Democrats and Republicans, who were unable to prevent a Russian premier, or then chairman of the USSR, from acting.

Now, third, that having been said, I want to associate myself with what Ranking Member Engel said in terms of our response now moving forward to support Ukraine. I believe there is more that we can be and should be doing. Clearly, we are in joint operations now with the three Baltic Republics as well as in Poland. I wish that we were doing more, and I am a cosponsor of legislation to do more in Ukraine, and I was hoping that possibly Mr. McFaul, you could speak to that more specifically what we could be doing now to bolster Ukraine and make sure that those who are Western looking succeed, because I agree, that would be one of the greatest things for American foreign policy.

Ambassador MCFAUL. So thank you for your question, and I agree. I want to associate myself with you in terms of that historical record. I think, in terms of Ukraine, I just want to underscore, again, more context, that I don't see consolidating democracy or strengthening markets in Ukraine as anti-Russian. When I was Ambassador, we had this argument frequently with senior members of the Russian Government, and we-our position, our administration's position, was you should be able to join whatever trade agreement you want, whatever treaty you want, as long as it doesn't infringe on other rights and responsibilities that you have in other organizations that you joined in terms of seeking win-win outcomes.

I think the idea of going back to some 19th century idea of spheres of influence makes no sense in the 21st century. The borders, you know, where I live in the Silicon Valley, the idea that somehow borders and geography are what makes countries rich or not is just, you know, that is a very outdated-- Mr. BOYLE. Very retrograde.

Ambassador MCFAUL. Yeah, I want to just really make that clear that this is not an anti-Russian policy that to support Ukrainian democracy or Ukrainian markets. And in that regard, I think the best investment that you all have supported with your support has been to help develop Ukrainian civil society. I think it has been a fantastic success story, that it cannot be done in other countries for other circumstances. But I think the pressure from society to make the government perform is the best way to try to help reform in Ukraine.

And it is working now. It is difficult, it is hard, it is not easy to correct 30 years of oligarchic corrupt capitalism. I want to underscore that. It is going to be a long process. It is going to take some electoral cycles, in my view, to change that, but I think that is the core. Support society, support independent media, and they will put the pressure on the government.

Mr. BOYLE. Let me-since I have time and now less than, in 50 seconds, let me just shift a bit. You know, there is something kind of self-centered in a sense that we always think when foreign policy actor does X, it is somehow because of something that the U.S. did or did not do. I tend to believe that a lot of Putin's actions in Crimea and eastern Ukraine have less to do with any U.S. policy and more to do with Russian domestic politics, and specifically, his standing, and I was wondering if any of you would like to speak to that. Agree or disagree?

Ambassador MCFAUL. Could I just briefly say--

Ambassador MATLOCK. Now--

Ambassador MCFAUL. Go ahead, Jack. Go ahead. I will go second.

Ambassador MATLOCK. I think one thing we tend to forget is that there is only one country that can solve Ukraine's problems, and that is Ukraine. The basic problem is that Ukraine is a deeply divided society.

When I was Ambassador to the Soviet Union, whenever I went to Ukraine, I always gave my speeches in Ukrainian language. I have been following things that happened in Ukraine since I was a high school student and did reporters on the role during the war. I know this country. And I also know that when they got independence, their borders were, to some degree, artificial.

**85**

Crimea had only been added by fiat without consulting anybody in the 1950s. Now-and so Ukraine-I went there to advise a group in the late 1990s on national security from-other former colleagues from our National Security Council, we were telling them how we organize our national security. The Ukrainians came back and said: Look, you are talking about foreign policy. Let me show you what our problem is. And they showed the sides of the last election, very evenly divided almost entirely on the west on one side and on the other side in the east and south.

Now-and this is in every election. Also, they had a constitution, which was not a Federal constitution, it was unitary. A President who won maybe by just 1 percentage of the vote named every governor. And you know where the violence started after the Maidan? It started in the west by them taking over the governorships. The corrupt President that they got rid of would never have been elected if Crimea had not been part of Ukraine.

There are a lot of issues here, a very deep history, and the basic problem is Ukraine. Yes, Russia has intervened, just as we take a very close interest in countries to us but--

Chairman ROYCE [presiding]. Yes, Ambassador,

but we have run over the time.

Ambassador MATLOCK [continuing]. The fact is the Ukrainians are going to have to solve it.

Chairman ROYCE. Right.

Ambassador MATLOCK. And our involvement tends to have a negative effect.

Chairman ROYCE. Yes, Ambassador. We are going to need to go to Mr. Ted Poe of Texas. Thank you.

Mr. POE. Thank you, Mr. Chairman. Thank you all for being here. Ambassador Matlock, I appreciate the fact that you are so knowledgeable, and you have looked at the whole issue with Russia as a historical point of view starting with really before World War I. I think we need to understand history, especially the way the Russians understand history so that we can move forward. I am not going to ask you a question, because if I ask you a question, it is like asking you the time, you will tell me how to make a watch, and so I am just going to make a couple of comments. I never thought I would see the day that in a committee hearing, we would have two former Ambassadors from the same region of the world mix it up together during the committee hearing. I think that is-it is a good thing. I am not being critical.

Ambassador MCFAUL. It is democracy, right?

Mr. POE. It is democracy. I think it is a good thing. Let's talk a little bit about Hitler.

The Russians moved into Georgia in 2008. I am always in the wrong place at the wrong time. I happened to be there a week after they invaded, and I saw the tanks up on the hill, and then in the West, we didn't do anything, and the tanks are still there and they have one-third of Georgia.

Crimea, the Russians took Crimea, their little green men, they moved into eastern Ukraine, chairman and I and some others were there right after the Russians came into eastern Ukraine, and they are still there. I just need a yes or no from the three of you.

Are the Russians going to stay in that one-third portion of Georgia, Crimea, and eastern Ukraine? Are they going to stay there or are they going to go home? Are they going to stay, Mr. Ambassador McFaul? Let's start on-I will start on the far left here. Are they going to stay in those areas?

Ambassador MCFAUL. My prediction is yes. You said one word. Mr. POE. One word. It is either yes or no.

Ambassador MCFAUL. I am a professor. I don't know how to give one word answers. Yes.

Mr. POE. Ambassador Matlock, just yes or no.

Ambassador MATLOCK. I think they are going to stay in those enclaves in Georgia, which the Georgians treat it the way the Serbs were treating Kosovo.

Mr. POE. All right.

Ambassador MATLOCK. And the problem has been--

Mr. POE. Mr. Ambassador, excuse me for interrupting.

Ambassador MATLOCK. Crimea--

Mr. POE. Crimea, are they going to stay in Crimea?

Ambassador MATLOCK. Will they stay? Most likely, unless--

Mr. POE. Answer the question.

Ambassador MATLOCK. Unless--

Mr. POE. Are they going to stay in Crimea?

Ambassador MATLOCK [continuing]. The majority of the people prefer to be in Ukraine. In that case, Crimea will become a liability, and there will be incentive to join with Ukraine.

Mr. POE. Eastern Ukraine, are they going to stay in eastern Ukraine?

Ambassador MATLOCK. They would be required to give Crimea autonomy--

Mr. POE. Mr. Ambassador, just answer the question.

Ambassador MATLOCK [continuing]. Which now they haven't been. I think a lot of--

Mr. POE. Mr. Ambassador, to stay in eastern Ukraine? The Russians in eastern Ukraine?

Ambassador MATLOCK. In eastern Ukraine, no. I think there was never an intent--

Mr. POE. Dr. Aron, what is your opinion?

Ambassador MATLOCK [continuing]. To take the Dombok. The Dombok--

Mr. POE. I have moved on to the next witness.

Ambassador MATLOCK. But they--

Mr. POE. I have moved on to the next witness, please, sir. I reclaim my time. My time.

Chairman ROYCE. I think just--

Ambassador MATLOCK. They will make sure that there is not an anti--

Mr. POE. I need some help, Mr. Chairman.

Ambassador MATLOCK. In charge of the Dombok.

Chairman ROYCE. I think my hearing is a little impaired, and I am not the only one with the difficulty sometimes of hearing, and so we will go to Dr. Aron.

Mr. POE. Thank you, sir.

Mr. ARON. Yes, on all three until the regime changes

Mr. POE. All right. The only other question I have time for is what do you think the Russians will do next? Where are they going? I think Putin finds an opportunity, he seizes it, and he moves in. People in Russia are nationalistic. His popularity skyrocketed when he went into Georgia and Ukraine. You know, I think he wants to be the next czar of Russia. I think that is probably what he is after, but where do you think they are going to go-Putin is going to move next?

Ambassador MCFAUL. I don't assume that he has a grand plan to go into this place and that place and the other. I think it is incumbent upon us to reduce the opportunities for him to do those things. I think Novorossiya has been a fantastic failure, for instance. What he tried to do in seizing territory in the eastern Ukraine has been a fantastic failure, and it is, in part, a failure because there was pushback. And that is why, you know, I go back to peace through strength. If we make sure that he has no doubt about our commitments to Estonia, Latvia, and Lithuania, that will keep the peace, and that is what I would want us to focus on as a way not because to confront Russia, but to keep the peace on that very precarious border.

Mr. POE. Dr. Aron, what is your opinion, future movement, if any, by Mr. Putin?

Mr. ARON. The most vulnerable is the Baltics, and of them, the most vulnerable, the Narva area between Russia and Estonia. And I agree with Mike, those are three NATO members now, and presumably, that is a deterrent.

But if the domestic situation requires it, I think Putin may try to expose NATO as a paper tiger, and have a great upsurge in domestic popularity. So that is a huge risk.

Chairman ROYCE. We need to go to Mr. Cicilline of Rhode Island.

Mr. CICILLINE. Thank you, Mr. Chairman. Thank you to our witnesses. I had an opportunity recently to travel with my good friend, Mr. Rohrabacher, to Moscow, and one of the meetings we had was at the Voice of America, Radio Free Europe. What I learned was very disturbing. The Russian Government, under the leadership of President Putin, had shut down all of the radio stations. I think there were 30 or so.

There was one station remaining that had a freestanding license, and then the Russian Government passed a law that required, if I am remembering this correctly, that it have the majority Russian ownership, so that license ultimately was revoked as well.

So Ambassador McFaul, it seems to me that in responding to this very sophisticated and very pervasive state-controlled media and propaganda machine, I think, really extraordinary, I think the best estimates are that they spend more than $450 million a year to broadcast to more than 30 million Russian speakers 24 hours a day, 7 days a week. What, if anything, are we doing, can we do to provide information that counters that narrative when the Voice of America and Radio Free Europe are basically precluded from providing information, or maybe that has changed since my visit? Ambassador MCFAUL. So I want Leon Aron to speak to this because he does serve on the BBG board and he knows these issues a lot better than I do, but I do want to just associate myself with what he said earlier in his testimony.

It is difficult for the United States Government to give money to reporters because that immediately will taint them. I know, you know, all the reporters, almost all the reporters in Russia, and if they were here today, the independent ones, they would say do not do that. We can't-we can't take your money. We need to be independent. What we can do is we can provide them with information, we can have strategic alliances with them to provide that, we can provide internships in our news organizations. We, at Stanford University, for instance, we have a Knight Fellowship program where we will soon have the former editor of Oktyabr as a visiting scholar because she was thrown out of her job.

And so those kinds of things, educational programs, I think, need to get much more attention. Because there are lots of, literally thousands of Russians, trying to figure out a way to contribute to their country that are now living in exile. These are the kind of opportunities that we should expand, but what we can do internally, I will let Leon answer that question, if he wants to.

Mr. ARON. Thanks very much, Mike. Thank you, sir. Just a brief comment. Russia is still not Iran or China. Social media are more or less free, and this is where the effort is going, because the generation we will want to affect is the generation of social media. And you know, as far as I know, BBG and the gruntees, that is the radios, are less of radios. They are more of TVs, they are more of Twitter, they are more of social media platforms, and I think there is hope there.

Mr. CICILLINE. Thank you. The second question I have is, one thing we saw a tremendous evidence of was the deterioration of the Russian economy, serious structural problems, falling oil prices, the Ukraine-related sanctions, and it is pretty clear the Kremlin has worked to preempt potential domestic discontent through this distraction of foreign interventions.

And my question really is, with the conflict in eastern Ukraine settling into a stalemate and the Russian military intervening in Syria last fall, how long can this kind of opportunistic strategy work? And what should we do to prepare against it? Maybe Ambassador McFaul, I can start with you?

Ambassador MCFAUL. So I agree with your analysis, and public opinion poll data out of Russia, even though it is very difficult to get accurate data, also concurs with that. I would just say historically and comparatively, we are not very good at predicting when declines and economic growth or depression leads to political change, and I would just remind you that I would never try to make a prediction based on that. But is there tension around that? Are people asking why are we in eastern Ukraine when, you know, our economic situation is getting worse? That question is being asked more and more there.

My view is we need to stay the course in terms of what the policy is. I want to lift sanctions on

Russian individuals and companies. I want to associate myself with that, if and when they do what they have signed up to do and their proxies have signed up to do in Mensk. It is just that simple. If you do this, then the sanctions will be lifted.

I find it very scary when people say sanctions aren't working, so let's lift them, or an idea that is floating around Europe right now, let's do partial sanctions for partial implementations. I think those are very bad ideas. Thank you.

Chairman ROYCE. We have luncheon with the Dalai Lama, so- and without objection, there are a couple of witness statements that I am going to include for the record.

And now we will go to Mr. Tom Marino of Pennsylvania.

Mr. MARINO. Thank you, Chairman. Excellent hearing. Gentlemen, I would like you to be as precise as possible. We all have something to do after this. I have three questions. Ambassador MCFAUL. I am not having lunch with the Dalai Lama. I wish I were.

Mr. MARINO. I am a former prosecutor. I don't have time for long winded answers. Let's go to number 1.

Ambassador McFaul, Putin obviously has a very big ego. People say to me he wants to be next General Secretary. I disagree with that. I think Putin wants to be the second Peter the Great, and the plan to make Russia a leading power, if not, the leading power with the world. What say you?

Ambassador MCFAUL. I agree.

Mr. MARINO. Great.

Ambassador MCFAUL. But I want Russia to be great, too. I personally think it would be in our national interest for Russia to be great. I do not believe the strategy he is seeking to achieve that objective is a smart one.

Mr. MARINO. Great. Okay. Dr. Aron, Bush's decision not to intervene in Georgia and Obama's decision not to intervene in Ukraine, I see that as signaling to Putin that the United States does not care to get involved in these foreign affairs, and as that, the U.S. will not challenge Putin, or NATO will not challenge Putin, will this allow him or signal to him that he could continue his expansionism?

Mr. ARON. Putin has not been made to pay for

his policies, definitely. The benefits, domestic political benefits, far supersede the price that he had to pay, either economically or militarily. There are ways to change this balance. It would require the things that Mike mentioned about Ukraine. I am also for arming Ukraine with strictly defensive weapons-but you're absolutely right. So long as his benefits, his domestic political benefits, exceed, far exceed the price that he pays politically and economically and militarily for his adventures, he will continue.

Mr. MARINO. Okay. And I am taking a gamble here, Ambassador Matlock. Please be very concise in your answer. Will Putin back off if the United States significantly increases its military strength and go back to the belief of Reagan through peace through strength?

Ambassador MATLOCK. I think he is more likely. I don't know that anybody can say precisely what he will do. He may not know. But the danger is, if we confront what he is doing militarily, which as yet, I think does not affect our national interest with military means, he can push us into another nuclear arms race. I think that is what we have to watch, because that is going to be very hard to deal with.

Mr. MARINO. Okay. Good point, Ambassador

Matlock. And then Dr. Aron, would you respond to that as well? Do we need to increase our military strength to keep Putin in check? Ambassador McFaul

Ambassador MCFAUL. Yes.

Ambassador MATLOCK. I think--

Mr. MARINO. Sir, Just a minute. Just a minute. I am asking Ambassador McCaul.

Chairman ROYCE. Ambassador McFaul, you are recognized. Ambassador MCFAUL. My answer is yes.

Mr. MARINO. Okay.

Ambassador MCFAUL. I support everything we are doing leading up to the Warsaw Summit.

Mr. MARINO. And I am sorry, I referred to you as McCaul.

Ambassador MCFAUL. Because you have a Member McCaul.

Mr. MARINO. I know. Dr. Aron.

Mr. ARON. I believe that Putin needs to see

some credible signs of paying more for his policies. Whether-I don't think we need to, you know, boost, you know, tremendously our military forces, but we need to look at specific instances where we can credibly threaten Putin to pay a higher price domestically, politically, for his adventures abroad.

Mr. MARINO. Just a little information. I am vice president of the NATO Parliamentary Assembly. I hear consistently, when I am in NATO meetings around the world, what is the United States going to do to put Putin in his place? I think perhaps he is one of the most dangerous people in the world, and gentlemen, I would love individually to have dinner with each one of you. I could learn so much. Thank you very much. I yield back.

Chairman ROYCE. Thank you, Mr. Marino, and I also want to thank the panel, the witnesses here today. We-and Jerry.

Mr. CONNOLLY. Thank you.

Chairman ROYCE. How are you?

Mr. CONNOLLY. Fine.

Chairman ROYCE. I am calling-I am going to recognize you. Go ahead.

Mr. CONNOLLY. Thank you, my friend. Thank you, Mr. Chairman. I want to pick up where my friend Mr. Marino left off. I am the head of the U.S. delegation to the NATO Parliamentary Assembly, and I have to say, I heard a lot of stuff from my friend from California and from Ambassador Matlock that would not, in any way, reflect the reality of our NATO partners across the board, with one or two exceptions. Boy, it would come as news to the Baltic republics that the Russians are peace-loving people who are just buzzing our ships in the Black Sea because we are too close to their littoral, because the Russians are buzzing them, and they are guilty of one thing, sovereign independence. That is what they are guilty of.

They are not doing anything provocative. In fact, the very last thing in the world they want to do is anything provocative. Explain that Russian behavior. The illegal annexation of the sovereign territory of the Ukraine, the Crimea, and now the illegal occupation. I was just in the Ukraine. Fighting goes on as we speak. People are dying because of Russian provocation. Russian subterfuge pretending these are Ukrainian nationalists and patriots who they have no control over.

We have already lost one commercial airliner in

that conflict. It was almost certainly downed. It was almost certainly downed at the loss of terrible civilian life over the sovereign territory of the Ukraine because of Russian provocation and Russian provocateurs, not Ukrainians, not Americans hating Russia. Russian behavior. Putin seems to be engaged in some kind of reestablishment of Russian hegemony in some kind of delusional czarist longing for some glorious past that really never existed, and that is very dangerous. It is also dangerous for Putin to misread U.S. resolve and NATO resolve. I worry about that.

History, in the last 200 years of this republic, is strewn with people who made that miscalculation, pushed us too far.

And Ambassador McFaul, I couldn't agree with you more with what you said earlier. That is Russia's responsibility. Maybe we have miscalculated an occasion. And we certainly shouldn't cloud the fact that there are areas of cooperation we appreciate. You know, we cooperate on the space station. We cooperated on JCPOA to a great contribution to world peace, as far as I am concerned. Although many of my friends on the other side of aisle, in fact, all of them opposed it, but it has been 100 percent complied with, and we are grateful to Russian participation and responsibility for at that.

But Putin seems to be pushing all the wrong-you know, the hot buttons with respect to the NATO alliance and to the United States. And I guess I would ask this, Ambassador McFaul: What is it you think Putin is trying to do? I mean, is it a testing of the system? Is it something more than that?

Ambassador MCFAUL. So thank you for your question, and I do agree that we need to stand with our allies. I think the idea of four new battalions in the east is the correct thing. Again, those battalions are not going to invade Russia. Come on, let's be honest about this. Only fools would think about doing that, and we are not foolish, but they are there in a defensive posture.

You know, my own view of why he did what he did is very contingent and circumstantial and emotional. I was still Ambassador, right? He didn't invade Ukraine when I was Ambassador. He invaded the day after I left. I want to point that out for the record. But the buildup was there, and it was in response to the collapse of the government in Kiev, right? It was to exact revenge over his ally falling there. It was not, in my view, some grand design to recreate the Soviet Union, and that, therefore, gives me hope that if we--

Mr. CONNOLLY. But let me interrupt you.

Ambassador MCFAUL. Yeah, please.

Mr. CONNOLLY. Again, I just came back from the Ukraine, but I also was in Kurdistan, I was also in Mongolia. My sense in Central Asia is deep anxiety about Russian intentions. There is a sense among those countries that that is precisely what he is up to, that this was not an isolated example.

Mr. Poe and I, the co-chairs of the Georgia caucus, I assure you the Georgians feel that this is about territorial reengagement and reexpansion after a period of contraction under Yeltsin and that period. And so I think there is real anxiety among lots of former eastern countries too and they are looking to our leadership to try to respond to it.

Mr. Chairman--

Chairman ROYCE. And I think on that point, Mr. Connolly, we really want to thank all the members. I want to thank the witnesses here, too. We had a great exchange of information. We may be following up with each of the witnesses here, and Tom Marino may be following up with you on dinner plans. So again, thank you, and we stand adjourned.

[Whereupon, at 12:10 p.m., the committee was adjourned.]

Appendix I
# THE AUTHOR

William Dunkerley is a media business analyst and Senior Fellow at American University in Moscow. He has worked on behalf of US interests in promoting press freedom in Eastern Europe and the former Soviet Union. He was commissioned by the International Federation of Journalists to analyze problems in certain Western press coverage of Russian issues. Mr. Dunkerley has been instrumental in shaping laws governing the media in Eastern Europe and Russia and has offered testimony to the United States Congress on media concerns. He has personally done intensive work in seven post communist countries, including interventions in seventeen different cities across all Russia. He is principal of William Dunkerley Publishing Consultants, and publisher of two industry monthlies, *Editors Only* and the *STRAT* newsletter.

Appendix II
# THIS SERIES

"Russia: Straight Talk on Hushed Issues" is a monograph series that looks behind the popular headlines and presents iconoclastic analyses. The books explain aspects of mainstream news that are either being distorted, glossed over, or hushed up.

The etiology of these media distortions is complex. Historically there was little harshness in the coverage of Yeltsin's misdeeds, perhaps a result of Western giddiness over the collapse of the Soviet Union.

When Putin entered the scene in 1999 the kid gloves came off. He was demonized. Russian tycoons who had been involved in skullduggery under Yeltsin found the new leader problematic.

Boris Berezovsky, one of the tycoons, carried

media attacks to new heights after fleeing  to London in 2001 to evade corruption charges. He packaged and distributed highly engaging news stories with associated graphics and interview opportunities to media outlets worldwide. Probably because of that convenience, they were readily accepted by the media unquestioningly despite their lack of factual bases.

Inexplicably, after Berezovsky's 2014 death, the stream of demonizing stories continued. Had Berezovsky's campaign just made an indelible impression that still taints the views of media and political leaders in the US and elsewhere? Or is there a new kingpin yet to be identified?

Regardless, many people have indeed formed beliefs based on the prevalence of distorted news and are committed to them. It would be unrealistic to think many of these folks will accept any contravening facts and analyses.

So the intention of this series is to give open-minded audiences in the US and other Western countries insights into misleading and fabricated reportage. That should allow them to arrive at more realistic and fact-based understandings, thus facilitating their serving more responsibly as members of our society. The intention is not to exonerate anyone who has been accused, but to point out that the accusers are liars and fabricators. (Note: Monographs in this series appear in no particular order.)

H.G. Wells once said: "Civilization is in a race between education and catastrophe."

But what is now unfolding in the theater of US-Russia relations is a race between catastrophe and utter disaster.

One entrant is the United States, and the other is Russia. Which country is on which side actually makes no difference. In this race, there are allegations, then sanctions, and then retributions for the previous actions. It is a self perpetuating loop.

This is a race in which the winner will personify either political buffoonery or plain stupidity. And which of the two is the victor will also make no difference. The main point for the rest of us is that this race will cause us all to lose.

As part of the "Russia: Straight Talk on Hushed Issues" monograph series, this book is dedicated to ending that foolish race, and to the concept of a safe, sustaining, and positive relationship between the United States and the Russian Federation.

Appendix III
# ACKNOWLEDGMENT

In the face of much media misinformation about Russia, I wish to acknowledge the effort and perseverance of all who have spoken and written the honest truth. They have shown great courage in bucking the unfortunate mainstream trend toward fabrication. Their work serves as an essential predicate to this book. --W.D.